Jim Arnosky

Thunder Birds

Nature's Flying Predators

STERLING

New York / London

FOR JIM BRETT

STERLING and the distinctive Sterling logo
are registered trademarks of Sterling Publishing Co., Inc.

Library of Congress Cataloging-in-Publication Data

Arnosky, Jim.
Thunder birds : nature's flying predators / by Jim Arnosky.
  p. cm.
Includes bibliographical references.
ISBN 978-1-4027-5661-0 (alk. paper)
  1. Birds of prey—Pictorial works. I. Title.
QL677.78.A76 2011
598.153—dc22

          2010019680

Lot #: 10 9 8 7 6 5 4 3 2 1
01/11

Published by Sterling Publishing Co., Inc.
387 Park Avenue South, New York, NY 10016
© 2011 by Jim Arnosky
Distributed in Canada by Sterling Publishing
c/o Canadian Manda Group, 165 Dufferin Street
Toronto, Ontario, Canada M6K 3H6
Distributed in the United Kingdom by GMC Distribution Services,
Castle Place, 166 High Street, Lewes, East Sussex, England BN7 1XU
Distributed in Australia by Capricorn Link (Australia) Pty. Ltd.
P.O. Box 704, Windsor, NSW 2756, Australia

The artwork for this book was created using acrylic paint and white chalk pencil.

Printed in China
All rights reserved

Sterling ISBN: 978-1-4027-5661-0

For information about custom editions, special sales, premium and
corporate purchases, please contact Sterling Special Sales Department
at 800-805-5489 or specialsales@sterlingpublishing.com.

Display lettering created by Georgia Deaver
Designed by Merideth Harte

CONTENTS

Introduction..5

Life-Size Eagles, Hawks, and Falcons.....7

Eagles, Hawks, and Falcons.........................11   FOLD OUT!

Life-Size Owls...12

Owls...15   FOLD OUT!

Vultures...17

Life-Size Herons and Egrets.....................19

Herons and Egrets......................................23   FOLD OUT!

Life-Size Pelicans.......................................24

Pelicans..27   FOLD OUT!

Loons, Cormorants, and Gannets............29

Nature's Flying Predators.......................31

Author's Note...32

More About Birds.......................................33

Metric Equivalents....................................33

GOLDEN EAGLE

LIFE-SIZE EAGLES, HAWKS, AND FALCONS

EAGLE

In flight eagles, hawks,
and falcons can be identified
by their silhouettes.

HAWK

8

FALCON

Introduction

Recently I set out with my wife, Deanna, who is my partner in adventure, to revisit many of our favorite places to find birds. Only *this* time around we were seeking only the largest and most powerful birds. We found many, from great tom turkeys to huge sandhill cranes that stood five feet tall. But the big birds I wanted to paint were the birds that hunted prey or caught fish—nature's flying predators.

I named my awesome subjects after the Thunderbird, a giant eaglelike Native American spirit that brought the thunder and lightning. My Thunder Birds are the biggest and strongest of birds that, with piercing talon or stabbing bill, reign fiercely over smaller wildlife. These birds make it easy to believe that dinosaurs never really died off, but are living today in the form of eagles, hawks, vultures, owls, herons, and pelicans.

Besides traveling to the wild places where we knew these birds would be, we also visited sanctuaries where wounded birds are being kept and cared for. Wherever birds were, we went to see them. Whenever we had a chance to learn more about them, we took advantage of it.

Marvel at these awe-inspiring creatures with us. I've painted many of them life-size and have made all of them as realistic as I possibly can so you will see the same light Deanna and I saw in their wild eyes.

Jim Arnosky

GOLDEN EAGLE
(Shown at half its actual size)

The largest feathers in a bird's wing are called the primaries. These are the stiff feathers that power flight.

A bird of prey you see in the daytime is either an eagle, falcon, hawk, or the hawklike, fish eating osprey. Of the four, eagles are the largest. A Bald Eagle, named so because of its white head, measures 36 inches from the top of its head to the tip of its tail and has a wingspan of 85 inches. (The Bald Eagle on the previous page is shown at half its actual size.) Golden Eagles are roughly the same size as Bald Eagles.

RED-SHOULDERED HAWK
Length: 23 inches
Wingspan: 40 inches

PEREGRINE FALCON
Length: 19 inches
Wingspan: 45 inches

BALD EAGLE

Eagles, Hawks, and Falcons

I once helped a biologist friend repair the wing of a wounded wild eagle. I held the eagle firmly by the feet as my friend sewed the damaged wing muscle. As I held the big bird's ankles together, the eagle bent its body toward my hands and probed at my skin with its large, curved beak, gently touching my knuckles and fingers. At first I was alarmed but my friend explained that an eagle uses its beak primarily to eat and to preen its feathers, not to defend itself. As long as I held the bird's powerful feet, preventing them from striking out and slashing us with their sharp talons (claws), we were safe.

Eagles, hawks, and falcons combine flight speed with strong grasping feet to subdue and kill a wide variety of small animals. They strike quickly from the sky, literally bowling their victims over by crashing into them and knocking them down.

Watching one of these big and powerful birds of prey catch and kill its food is one of the most spectacular and shocking sights you can witness in nature. Seeing it all up close through binoculars or through a telephoto camera lens can raise the hair on the back of your neck.

Eagle foot shown actual size.

OSPREY

Length: 22 inches
Wingspan: 64 inches

The Osprey, or Fish Hawk as it is sometimes called, has a flight
silhouette and body size similar to a hawk's, but has a wingspan nearly
as large as an eagle's. Extra-large wings enable an Osprey to lift a heavy
fish out of the water and carry it away to be killed and eaten.

SNOWY OWL

Owls

We can only imagine the terror a mouse or rabbit experiences when fleeing an eagle or a hawk attack, as it is quickly overcome by the sound and fury of wing beats. In sharp contrast, animals killed by owls are taken unaware, never knowing what hit them.

An owl's wing feathers are soft and are separated at the tips to sift air rather than slice through it. This makes owl wings silent in flight. An owl's feathered feet also have soft edges for silent flight. Prey animals are taken suddenly and without warning in the midst of whatever they happen to be doing. Only in bright moonlight might an owl's intended victim sense what is coming, when it sees the hunter's large shadow moving across the ground.

At night in the forest, while I was taking flash photos of owls, one of the big birds swooped down toward me from behind, lightly brushing my head with its wings. I felt it and then I saw it, but I never heard it coming.

Owl wing feathers

An owl's feathered foot

The easiest way to identify an owl is by its face. All of these owl faces are shown life-size. Although large owls will kill and eat birds, rabbits, snakes, stray cats, and even skunks, rodents are their main prey. If you live in a city with a park, you most likely have resident owls feeding through the night, keeping the rodent population in check.

BARRED OWL
Length: 20 inches
Wingspan: 48 inches

Barred Owls live in the swamps and woodlands of the United States and Canada.

BARN OWL
Length: 20 inches
Wingspan: 44 inches

An owl of wide open country and farmland where it inhabits barns and sheds as well as cliffs and caves.

GREAT HORNED OWL
Length: 25 inches
Wingspan: 50 inches

Great Horned Owls live in forests, woodlots, and city parks.

14

LIFE-SIZE OWLS

GREAT GRAY OWL
Length: 33 inches
Wingspan: 62 inches

Owls of the northern evergreen
forests of the United States
and Canada.

SNOWY OWL
(Previous page)
Length: 25 inches
Wingspan: 50 inches

Snowy Owls, like the one shown
at left, live in the northern United
States and Canada and in the
Arctic tundra.

BLACK VULTURES

Vultures

Drying after a shower

Vultures do not usually kill to eat. They feed on carrion—animals they find that are already dead. In North America there is the Turkey Vulture, named for its red, turkey-like head, and the Black Vulture, whose head is gray.

Vultures find food visually or by smell. The odor of carrion rises in columns of warm air called thermals. Vultures soar high, kept aloft by these same thermals and circle in the sky until they smell the scent or see carrion to eat.

When a vulture finds food, it must eat it wherever it may be. Vulture feet are not strong enough to lift and move things. This is why we see vultures feeding on roadkill right on the road, flying off and returning to their food each time a vehicle passes. To eat, a vulture uses its sharp beak to rip open holes in a dead animal's skin. Then it pokes its head inside to tear away bits of flesh. Vultures have naked heads, which are cleaner than feathers for feeding inside an animal carcass. The vulture's head at the far left is shown life-size.

In the Everglades, Deanna and I saw a flock of Black Vultures feeding on an old alligator that had died. The big birds tore holes in the soft skin on the alligator's belly and fed on the flesh inside. In less than a week, they had reduced the eight-foot alligator to a floating skin bag of bones.

Black Vulture

Turkey Vulture

Identifying vultures by shape and pattern:

Black Vulture
Length: 25 inches
Wingspan: 56 inches

Turkey Vulture
Length: 27 inches
Wingspan: 70 inches

LIFE-SIZE HERONS AND EGRETS

AMERICAN BITTERN
Length: 27 inches
Wingspan: 39 inches

The American Bittern, a close relation of herons and egrets, blends so well with its surroundings that it is rarely seen. Listen for the Bittern's strange sounding call: *ka-GOON-cha* to know whether one is in your area.

LITTLE BLUE HERON
Length: 24 inches
Wingspan: 40 inches

The Little Blue Heron does most of its hunting near the water's edge searching for small crustaceans, fish, amphibians, and insects.

BLACK CROWNED NIGHT HERON
Length: 25 inches
Wingspan: 44 inches

These are the only herons whose females look different from the males. Female Night Herons are mottled brown in color.

Egrets and herons
can stretch their
necks as long as
their body length.

GREAT EGRET
Length: 38 inches
Wingspan: 55 inches

Great Egrets can be
distinguished from Great
White Herons by their
legs. Great Egrets have
black legs. Great White
Herons have yellow legs.

GREEN HERON
Length: 18 inches
Wingspan: 24 inches

GREAT BLUE HERON AND BROWN WATER SNAKE

Herons and Egrets

Of all the birds that I watch, I love watching herons and egrets the most. There is such suspense in the way they slowly stalk fish in shallow water, bill downward, long neck poised to strike. The eyes of herons and egrets are set in such a way that they can look downward to watch for prey or forward to give the birds binocular vision and the depth perception necessary to spear a moving target in the water. Herons and egrets will wade in water as deep as their legs are long, but never so deep that they wet their feathers or lose their footing on the bottom. Afloat, they are easy prey for big snapping turtles or alligators.

The largest of these birds is the Great Blue Heron, standing over forty inches tall. A Great Blue Heron can catch and swallow a fish its own weight or a snake as long as the heron is tall.

Deanna spotted a Great Blue Heron with a water snake that hung down to the heron's feet. A snake that size would have had to be killed by heavy blows and chops to the head from the heron's big spear-shaped beak. The lifeless snake was swallowed whole, headfirst, a little at a time, until it was all down.

forward-facing eyes

Great Blue Heron footprint in soft mud.

You can recognize a flying heron or egret by its long bill and long legs.

GREAT WHITE HERON
Length: 50 inches
Wingspan: 75 inches

In the United States,
Great White Herons are
found only in Florida.

After spearing its prey, a heron or egret will flip and turn the
animal in its beak in order to swallow it head first. Swallowing
animals head first lessens any chance of their escape and, in the
case of fish, prevents fins from spreading open and sticking in the
swallower's throat.

GREAT BLUE HERON
Length: 45 inches
Wingspan: 70 inches

Heron and egret feet are large with long toes that spread wide for good footing on soft mud.

A fourth (hind) toe is not shown here.

BROWN PELICAN

Pelicans

We were sitting in the shade of a rustic little hut on the edge of a fishing wharf when the sky suddenly clouded over and it began to rain, then pour. The heavy drops made loud popping sounds as they hit the tin roof of our shelter. Outside in the rain a Brown Pelican perched on a dock piling and began swaying rhythmically forward and backward, side to side, with its head facing upward and bill wide open. The pelican was catching raindrops to quench its thirst! Suddenly, I wanted to go out in the downpour and drink rainwater too.

A Brown Pelican (50 inches long, with a wingspan of 80 inches) is the kind of bird that makes you wonder what it would be like to live outdoors in the sun and wind, weathering every storm. What is it like to go flying over the ocean waves and diving for your supper?

When a Brown Pelican sees a fish in the water, it simply drops down headfirst to catch it. As soon as the pelican hits the surface it opens its bill, filling its throat pouch with water, which widens its mouth in order to trap its catch.

Brown Pelicans are coastal dwellers. American White Pelicans can be found on seacoasts and also inland on large freshwater lakes, marshes, and rivers. American White Pelicans are not divers. They catch fish as a flock by swimming close together and driving whole schools of frantic fish into shallow water where they can be scooped up one or two at a time into the pelicans' bills.

Pelicans have the largest bills of all birds. The top bill is made of highly porous bone; it weighs only three or four ounces. The bottom bill is pliable and opens wide to engulf fish. The throat pouch is made of flexible, stretchable skin.

Catching raindrops.

Diving for a fish.

Throat pouch expanding.

White Pelicans fishing together.

LIFE-SIZE PELICANS

During breeding season, the male American White Pelican grows a keel-like bill plate on the top of its bill.

At five feet from the tip of its enormous bill to the end of its tail feathers, and with a wingspan of just under 10 feet, the American White Pelican ranks as one of the largest birds in North America.

AMERICAN WHITE PELICAN
Length: 60 inches
Wingspan: 110 inches

Great Cormorant
Length: 36 inches
Wingspan: 60 inches

Common Loon
(life-size)
Length: 34 inches
Wingspan: 58 inches

Double-crested Cormorant
Length: 33 inches
Wingspan: 50 inches

Northern Gannet
(life-size)
Length: 36 inches
Wingspan: 72 inches

Loons, Cormorants, and Gannets

Pelicans dive just under the water surface for fish. They are not deep divers. The deep-diving birds are the loons, cormorants, and gannets. Gannets are strictly saltwater birds. Loons and cormorants are found in saltwater and in freshwater.

The loon is the deep-diving champ, swimming down 200 feet or more to catch swift fish, which are stabbed, speared, or grasped in the loon's sturdy pointed bill. You can get a sense of just how far and fast a loon can swim underwater by noting the time and place that the bird submerges and the time and place that it resurfaces.

Loons have a weirdly human-sounding call: *WaahooohAAA!* They are heavy birds that require a long flyway to become airborne, so loons will only land on bodies of water large enough to allow them to take off again.

Cormorants do not dive as deep as loons, but they dive deep enough to catch bottom-feeding fish and crustaceans. Neither loons nor cormorants plunge from the air to dive in water. They dive from a floating position and power underwater, propelled by their large webbed feet. Cormorants will often "snorkel" with body afloat and head poked underwater to look around before diving.

Gannets are almost as large as pelicans, but are more streamlined and are much more spectacular divers. Gannets dive from heights of 150 feet, and they hit the water with a tremendous splash. You can identify a gannet simply by the height of its dive and the size of its splash. They dive down as deep as 40 feet and swim into schools of herring, slashing and cutting the fish with their sharp bills.

Loon diving.

Cormorant snorkeling.

All diving birds have strong, short legs set far back on the body and large webbed feet.

OSPREY WITH TROUT

Nature's Flying Predators

I love being out in open country and seeing an eagle or a hawk wheeling slowly overhead. And when one alights on a tree, I run to get a closer look. If I'm lucky, the bird will stay awhile and I'll see it ruffle the feathers on its back or spread its wings for a few audible flaps. I wonder about everything birds do, and I want you to wonder, too.

The next time you watch an osprey carrying a freshly caught fish, try to imagine the bird's actual size. How big and heavy would it be if it perched on your outstretched arm? How wide would its wings spread? How long and curved and sharp are its talons? And how many fish must it catch to feed itself and its family back in the nest?

Birds know a freedom of movement and space that we can only imagine. They have a limitless sky in which to fly and the whole world to come down to. Up high, they can see the patchwork of the landscape, the expanse of the sea, and the broad curve of the horizon. They climb on air and ride the wind. They hover, flap, glide, and soar. Everything about them is fascinating. And the big predatory birds fascinate us the most. Nature's flying predators are magnificent creatures of the earth and water as well as of the sky.

AUTHOR'S NOTE

The life-size paintings in this book, done in acrylic paint and white chalk pencil, are the result of many years of research in the field and thousands of miles of travel. Here are some of the places Deanna and I have visited again and again in our search for America's birds.

We encourage you to include these amazing locations on your lifetime list of places to see for yourself.

Attwater Prairie Chicken NWR*, TX
Bear River NWR, UT
Bombay Hook NWR, DE
Chincoteague NWR, VA
Crocodile Lake NWR, FL
Custer State Park, SD
Dead Creek Wildlife Management Area, VT
Everglades National Park, FL
Four Holes Swamp Audubon Sanctuary, SC
Great Dismal Swamp NWR, VA
Hawk Mountain Sanctuary, PA
Iroquois NWR, NY
J.N. "Ding" Darling NWR, FL
Loxahatchee NWR, FL
Merritt Island NWR, FL
Middle Creek Wildlife Area, PA
Missisquoi NWR, VT

Mississippi Sandhill Crane NWR, MS
Montezuma NWR, NY
Okefenokee NWR, GA
Sabine NWR, LA
Salt Plains NWR, OK
Saguaro National Park, AZ
St. Augustine Alligator Farm and Zoological Park, FL
San Pedro River Riparian National Conservation Area, AZ
Savannah NWR, SC
Tallgrass Prairie Preserve, OK
Tonto National Forest, AZ
Vermont Institute of Natural Science, VT
Yellowstone National Park, WY

*NWR stands for "National Wildlife Refuge"

You can learn more about these and other great bird places by searching the Web for National Wildlife Refuges, National Parks, State Parks, Wildlife Management Areas, and Audubon Bird Sanctuaries. No matter where you go, there are big, powerful birds to see. Watch the water and the sky for the Thunder Birds.

MORE ABOUT BIRDS

Alderfer, Jonathan. *National Geographic Complete Book of Birds*. New York: National Geographic, 2005.

Arnosky, Jim. *Crinkleroot's Guide to Knowing the Birds*. New York: Simon & Schuster, 1997.

Arnosky, Jim. *Watching Water Birds*. New York: National Geographic Children's Books, 2002.

Dunn, Jon L. *National Geographic Illustrated Birds of North America*, Folio Edition. New York: National Geographic, 2009.

Floyd, Ted. *Smithsonian Field Guide to the Birds of North America*. New York: HarperCollins, 2008.

Frost, Paul D. *Birds of Prey*: Majestic Masters of the Skies. New York: Parragon, Inc., 2008.

Laubach, Christyna M. *Raptor! A Kid's Guide to Birds of Prey*. North Adams, MA: Storey Publishing, 2002.

Markle, Sandra. *Vultures*. Minneapolis, MN: Lerner Publications, 2006.

National Audubon Society. *Field Guide to North American Birds*. New York: Alfred A. Knopf, 1994.

Parry-Jones, Jemima. *Eyewitness: Eagle and Birds of Prey*. New York: Dorling Kindersley Limited, 2000.

Sill, Cathryn. *About Raptors*. Atlanta, GA: Peachtree Publishers, 2010.

Swan, Erin Pembrey. *Pelicans, Cormorants, and Their Kin*. New York: Franklin Watts/Scholastic, Inc., 2002.

Vuilleumier, Francois, ed. *Birds of North America (American Museum of Natural History)*. New York: Dorling Kindersley Limited, 2009

METRIC EQUIVALENTS
(TO THE NEAREST 0.1 CM OR 0.01 M)

inches	cm	feet	meters	pounds	kilograms
1	2.5	1	0.30	1	0.45
2	5.1	2	0.61	2	0.91
3	7.6	3	0.91	10	4.5
4	10.2	4	1.22	100	45
5	12.7	5	1.52	200	91
6	15.2	6	1.83	500	227
7	17.8	7	2.13	1000	454
8	20.3	8	2.44		
9	22.9	9	2.74		
10	25.4	10	3.05		
11	27.9				
12	30.5